W9-CPG-730

Map My Neighborhood

by Jennifer Boothroyd

first step nonfiction

Lerner Publications · Minneapolis

LERNER

SOURCE

Expand learning beyond the printed book. Download free, complementary educational resources for this book from our website, www.lerneresource.com.

Copyright © 2014 by Lerner Publishing Group, Inc.

All rights reserved. International copyright secured. No part of this book may be reproduced, stored in a retrieval system, or transmitted in any form or by any means—electronic, mechanical, photocopying, recording, or otherwise—without the prior written permission of Lerner Publishing Group, Inc., except for the inclusion of brief quotations in an acknowledged review.

The images in this book are used with the permission of: © Prisma/SuperStock, p. 4; © JTB Photo/SuperStock, p. 5; © iStockphoto.com/Jonathan Cohen, p. 6; © iStockphoto.com/Chad Thomas, p. 7; © Laura Westlund/Independent Picture Service, pp. 8, 10, 11, 12, 13, 14, 15, 16, 17, 18, 19; © iStockphoto.com/seamartini, p. 9; © Todd Strand/Independent Picture Service, p. 21.

Front cover: © Laura Westlund/Independent Picture Service.

Main body text set in ITC Avant Garde Gothic Std Medium 21/25.
Typeface provided by Adobe Systems.

Lerner Publications Company
A division of Lerner Publishing Group, Inc.
241 First Avenue North
Minneapolis, MN 55401 USA

For reading levels and more information, look up this title at www.lernerbooks.com.

Library of Congress Cataloging-in-Publication Data

Boothroyd, Jennifer, 1972–
    Map my neighborhood / by Jennifer Boothroyd.
        p.   cm. – (First step nonfiction—Map it out)
    Includes index.
    ISBN 978–1–4677–1111–1 (lib. bdg. : alk. paper)
    ISBN 978–1–4677–1740–3 (eb pdf)
    1. Maps—Juvenile literature. I. Title.
GA130.B58 2014
526—dc23   2012037533

Manufactured in the United States of America
3-42921-13075-9/12/2016

PUBLIC LIBRARY DISTRICT OF COLUMBIA

Table of Contents

Grandma is coming for a visit.

She has never seen my
neighborhood.

I will make her a **map**.

A map shows the **location**
of places or things.

Planning a Map

home

library

store

park

street

school

I made a list of places to put on the map.

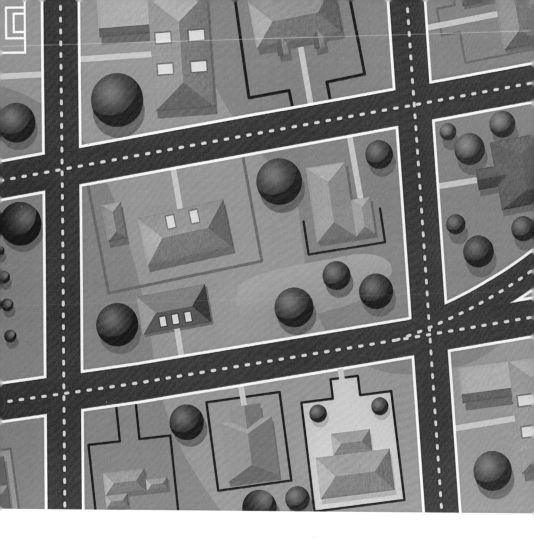

A map has **symbols**. They stand for places.

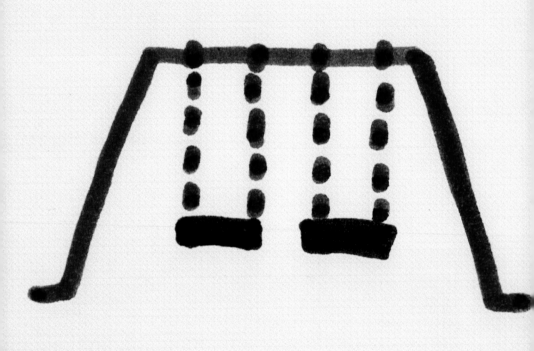

This is my symbol for the park.

This is my symbol for the store.

I made a **key**. It tells what my symbols mean.

I drew my home.

Key

home

library

store

park

street

school

I drew my street. The road
runs north and south.

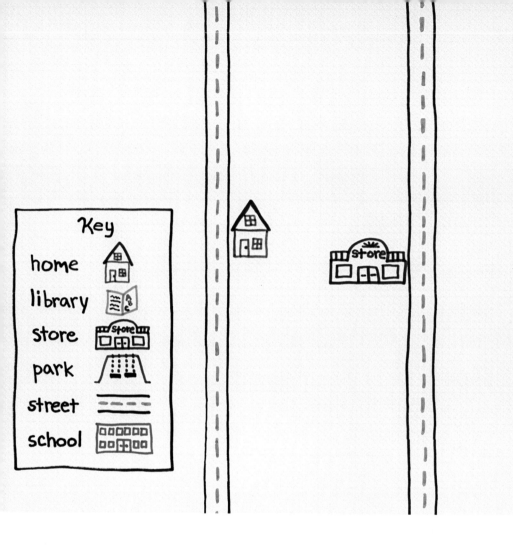

The store is on a different street. It is east of my home.

My school is south.

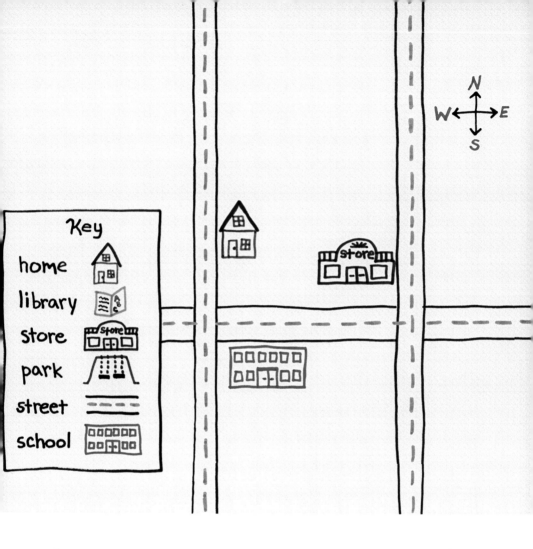

I drew a **compass rose** in the corner.

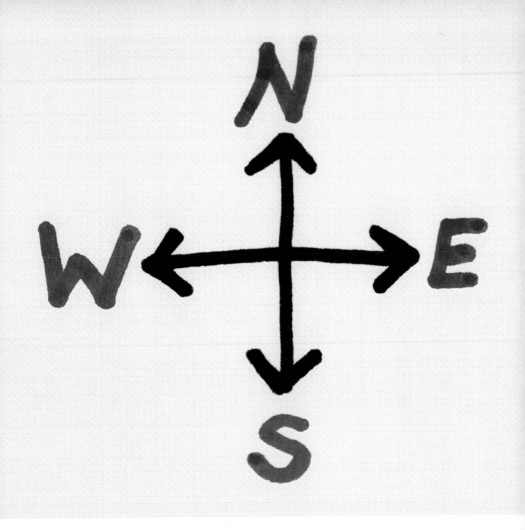

It shows the **directions** on a map.

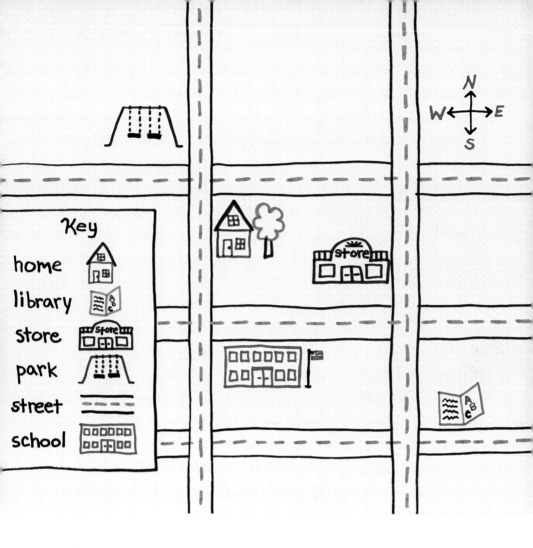

All done! I hope Grandma
likes my map.

How to Make a Neighborhood Map

1. List all the places you want on the map.
2. Make a symbol for each place.
3. Make a key to show what each symbol means.
4. Which place is in the middle of your neighborhood? Draw the symbol for the place in the center of the map.
5. Draw the rest of the symbols in their locations.
6. Add a compass rose.

Fun Facts

- Neighborhoods are different sizes. They have homes, stores, places of worship, and other buildings.

- Some neighborhoods are filled only with places to live. People have to travel miles to visit a store or the library.

- People living in a neighborhood are called neighbors.

Glossary

compass rose – a symbol that
shows directions on a map

directions – one of four main
points of a compass. The
four directions are north,
south, east, and west.

key – the part of a map that
explains the symbols

location – where something is

map – a drawing that shows
where places are

neighborhood – an area of a
city or a town where people
live

symbols – things that stand for
something else

Index

JAN 0 3 2017